Titus Maccius Plautus

The Pot of Gold
(Aulularia)

Translated, with the missing part of the final act completed,
by David Bolton.

Published by Lulu Books

2019

Copyright by David Bolton

ISBN 978-0-244-22394-6

Terms for the performance of this play may be obtained from
David Bolton at dgbolton0@gmail.com.

All translations in this edition, including the introductory sections (unless
specifically attributed) are by David Bolton.

Colour: #C3161C

Contents

Titus Maccius Plautus

References in the works of Cicero suggest that Plautus was born c254 BC and died c184 BC. Festus (2nd century AD) says he was born in Sarsina in Umbria in Northern Italy.

Few details of his life are known. There is even doubt about his name: Maccius Plautus could be interpreted as 'Clown Flatfoot'. As to his life, some evidence comes from Aulus Gellius, who, referring to the works of Varro, says "Varro and many others have recorded that he wrote *Saturio*, *Addictus* and a third comedy, the name of which now escapes me, whilst working in a bakery, since, having lost in trade all the money he earned whilst employed in the theatre, he returned destitute to Rome and, to earn a livelihood, he found a job with a baker turning a mill, called a 'hand-mill'."[1] His 'employment in the theatre' presumably would include general work as a stagehand and constructing scenery. His later work in the bakery would have been low-paid, and would have involved operating a mill with two handles, requiring two men to push or turn them. The strength of Gellius' evidence is disputed: it is suggested that the story may have attached itself to Plautus since characters in his plays are often threatened with 'working the mill'. Conversely, of course, this threat could appear frequently in Plautus because of his own personal experience.

Ancient Sarsina was situated in a rural area of North Eastern Italy and Plautus was perhaps unlikely to become acquainted there with either the theatre or, more especially, the Greek theatre. Gellius says of him that 'he returned ... to Rome' after his failed commercial venture.

---

[1] Aulus Gellius, *Noctes Atticae* III. 3

How Plautus developed his Latin style, learnt Greek and studied Greek literature is unknown. Perhaps, he left Sarsina for Rome, got caught up in the theatre, and developed the necessary skills in the process.

The twenty-one extant comedies (some being fragmentary) are considered to have been written in the last twenty or twenty-five years of his life, that is, after, say, 209 BC until his death in 184 BC, that is, from around age 45 or 50 to his death at the age of about 70 [1].

The dates of the first performances of most plays, however, are uncertain. *Saturio*, *Addictus* and the third comedy referred to by Gellius appear to have been early works. Gellius adds: "There are about one hundred and thirty comedies ascribed to Plautus, but L. Aelius, a most learned man, judged only twenty-five to be his. But there is no doubt that those that do not seem to have been written by Plautus whilst attributed with his name, were by ancient playwrights, and were reworked and polished by him. Consequently they smack of the Plautine style"[2].

---

[1] Discussed by G. E. Duckworth, *Nature of Roman Comedy: a Study in Popular Entertainment*

[2] Aulus Gellius, *Noctes Atticae* III. 3

Roman comedy

The Greek Old Comedy, performed at the Athenian Dionysia and represented by Aristophanes is associated with the fifth century BC. Little is known of later comedy production until the late fourth century, when Greek New Comedy emerged. The choruses of the earlier Greek plays fell away and dramas took more the format of modern plays. Stock characters emerged: young men in love, slaves cleverer than their masters, female slaves who turn out to be well-born, braggart soldiers, irascible old men who complain about their wives, hungry parasites and greedy slave dealers.

The writers of these comedies include Menander, Philemon and Diphilus of the late fourth and early third centuries. Roman playwrights such as Plautus and Terence took the original plays of these playwrights and did not simply translate them but rewrote them. As Plautus says of the play *Casina*, in its Prologue, "In Greek, the play is called *Clerumenoe*, which means 'The drawing of lots'. Diphilus wrote the play in Greek, and later, Plautus, starting afresh, in Latin". Plautus is known to have reworked the plays of Menander, Philemon, Diphilus and also the minor playwright Demophilus.

Whilst the action of each play takes place in some Greek city (eg. Athens, Sicyon, Epidamnus or Epidaurus), and the actors wore Greek clothes, the references remain Roman: Roman gods, the Roman forum, Rome's magistrates, laws and law courts, the Roman Senate and places in and around Rome.

The Greek clothes of the actors would in particular have included the *pallium* or cloak for the (non-slave) male characters (hence this form of play or *fabula* was called '*palliata*'). Male characters generally wore tunics as the basic item of clothing. There is some debate as to whether masks were worn; being comedy, there would no doubt be some elements of outlandish appearance.

At least part of each play was given musical accompaniment: the surviving texts of the six plays of Terence state that one Flaccus Claudi performed at each first performance of each play on a variety of reed flutes. Commentators have examined the metrical structure of the plays. There is some consensus that some of the dialogue was spoken, but that much of the dialogue and speeches were 'sung', that is, either chanted or sung as recitative to the accompaniment of the flute. There do not appear, however, to have been 'arias' or songs as such.

The plays were performed during Games held as part of religious festivals. The plays of Terence give details of the Games at which his plays were first performed. These include the *Ludi Megalenses* in honour of the Goddess Cybele also known as *Magna Mater*, the *Ludi Romani* in honour of Jupiter, and the Funeral Games held for L. Aemilius Paulus. In other words, they were held at each of the annual *Ludi* and at other one-off important occasions such as a public funeral.

The actors will often have been slaves, who may have been beaten if their performance was poor. They certainly asked for applause at the end of each play. The Epilogue to Plautus' *Cistellaria* (*The Casket*) sums this up:

"Audience, don't expect the actors to appear on stage again: that's the end of the play! They're taking their costumes off now, and the actor who forgot his lines will be given a beating, and the one who didn't will get a drink.

All that remains, is for you, in time honoured fashion, to give us a round of applause."

Roman theatres developed from wooden structures to elaborate stone ones. For the actors, there appear to have been entrances from the wings, a central entrance, and further entrances on either side of the central entrance. This arrangement conveniently fits the set of most Roman comedies, which often present two houses with a street running in front of or between them.

The plays had to appeal to a broad audience. They were studied by literary men such as Varro and Cicero, but they also had to appeal to the Roman populace at large, many of whom would have little or no literary interest, and many of the foreigners in Rome would have little Latin. They also had competition from rival, non-literary performances: Terence tells of the problems he once encountered: "As soon as I began to show it [my play], the challenges of boxers (also the expectation of some tight-rope dancers), the crowds of followers, the noise and the shouts of women, made me finish with the play before the conclusion. I began to apply my old methods to this new play as a trial. I presented it afresh. The first act was well received. Meanwhile, a rumour circulated that a gladiatorial contest was to be held: the crowds gathered; they jostled and shouted and fought for their place."[1]

Yet the Latin of Plautus and Terence is well crafted (though idiomatic) and often in complex verse form. Perhaps, then, it is possible to underestimate the Roman audiences, who must in fact have appreciated the literary aspects of the plays.

---

[1] Terence, *Hecyra*, Prologus (II)

The broad appeal required of his plays may have led Plautus in particular to be influenced by two earlier Italian theatrical traditions: the Atellane plays and the form of play developed by Livius Andronicus. Livy says that in the mid-fourth century 'scenic games' were introduced; the actors were from Etruria and there were no words but only dancing to the flute; these were imitated locally with the introduction of comic verses and actions to suit the words; this became an accepted form; but then, Livius Andronicus first produced a play with a plot; his plays had spoken dialogue, but also large sections delivered with words 'sung' or chanted to flutes; whilst such plays were left to actors, young men again performed comic verses, known as *'exodia'*, or 'after-verses', which were strung together to form 'Atellane plays'; these were of Oscan origin.[1]

St Jerome read Plautus at the end of the fourth century AD; but Plautus received little interest in the Middle Ages, unlike Terence who continued to be copied and read. Plautus resurfaced, however, and influenced Shakespeare, whose *Comedy of Errors* reflects *Menaechmi*, Ben Jonson, whose *The Case is Altered* reflects *Aulularia* and *Captivi*, Molière, whose *L'Avare* is based on *Aulularia*, and many others including Stephen Sondheim's *A Funny Thing Happened on the Way to the Forum* (*Pseudolus*, *Miles Gloriosus* and *Mostellaria*).

[1] Livy, *History of Rome* VII. 2

The Pot of Gold (Aulularia)

There is tentative evidence that *The Pot of Gold* was based on a play by Menander: there is reference to an unknown Menander play in which a man fears the smoke escaping from his chimney (see Pythodicus' view of Euclio in 2.4). The original play is equally tentatively dated at 317 to 307 BC on the basis of a reference in *The Pot of Gold* to the 'Minister for Women' – an actual office in Athens during those dates.

The original Greek play was set in Athens and Plautus retained this setting for *The Pot of Gold*. The Gods referred to in the play, however, are Roman and Lyconides' encounter with Phaedria took place during the Roman Festival of Ceres. The Prologue is spoken by the 'Spirit of the Hearth', denoted in the text as *Lar familiaris*: homes were considered to be protected by guardian deities, the *Lares et Penates*. *Lares* were of Etruscan origin, *Penates* of Latin origin. Images of the deity or deities often, but by no means always, stood on the hearth in a small shrine in the protected home.

The Pot of Gold introduces an old miser and an old bachelor. The old bachelor, typically of older male comedy characters, when contemplating marriage prefers a young girl to a lady of more advanced years. The housekeeper, Staphyla, does not so much outwit her master (as slaves generally do in Roman comedies) as show more understanding: she knows of Phaedria's plight and cares for her. Strobilus, on the other hand, does outwit Euclio, but is inevitably caught out by his master Lyconides.

The set of *The Pot of Gold*, as was common in Roman comedies, featured two houses with a street running in front of or between them.

The Prologue is typical of Roman comedy: whilst it lacks the introductory passages designed to warm the audience up, it sets the scene, ensures the audience understand at the outset what the play is about, and enables the playwright to launch straight into the plot – thus capturing and maintaining the interest of a possibly fickle audience.

The characters names are derived from Greek, and may have amusing derivations: 'Staphyla', for example, means a 'bunch of grapes'; of the cooks, 'Congrio' suggests a conger-eel and 'Anthrax' is the Greek word for coal; the name of the flute girl Eleusium, suggesting the Greek town of Eleusis, is of neuter gender, as is often the case with slave girls in Roman comedy, particularly ones of doubtful morality.

The bulk of the last act is missing from extant texts. The only evidence for how the play concludes is supplied in the *Argumenta*, the two 'Plots' supplied with the texts of the play. In these, it is clear that Lyconides recovers the gold and returns it to Euclio and that Euclio gives both the gold and Phaedria's hand in marriage to Lyconides. In the version of the final act presented in this book, the Spirit of the Hearth makes a reappearance and helps persuade Euclio that Phaedria and the gold are best bestowed on Lyconides. The logic of this ending is that the Spirit of the Hearth says in the Prologue that he wants to help the devout Phaedria and that it is he who is engineering the course of events. Why then should he not put in an appearance to finish the job off?

The Pot of Gold
(Aulularia)

(The Plots and Dramatis Personae set out on pages 17 and 19 derive from the transmitted editions of the play.)

The Plot (1) [1]

An old miser, Euclio, a man so distrustful he would barely trust himself, finds a pot full of golden treasure buried in his own home. He hides it again deep in the ground and watches over it with a demented anguish. Lyconides has made his daughter pregnant; but in the meantime, an old bachelor, Megadorus, persuaded by his sister to marry, asks for the hand of this miser's daughter. The hard-hearted miser grudgingly gives his consent, and, fearing for his pot of gold, moves it from his house and hides it in various places. The slave of Lyconides the young girl's lover, laid a trap for the miser. Lyconides himself begs his uncle Megadorus to give up the girl to himself to marry since he is in love with her. Soon, Euclio, who has lost his pot of gold through trickery, unexpectedly finds it again and joyfully betroths his daughter to Lyconides.

The Plot (2)

A pot of gold is found by Euclio.
Under much stress, he watches over it.
Lyconides with child his daughter makes;
Urged on, though, Megadorus wants her hand,
Lithely orders cooks prepare the wedding feast.
An anguished Euclio hides his pot outside –
Revealed, though! Lyconides's slave
It steals. Lyconides tells Euclio,
And from him gets his daughter and his gold.

---

[1] The Plots are thought not to have been written by Plautus.

Dramatis Personae[1]

Spirit of the Hearth, the Prologue

Euclio, an old man

Staphyla, an old woman

Eunomia, a married woman

Megadorus, an old man

Pythodicus, a slave

Congrio ⎱
          ⎰ cooks
Anthrax ⎰

Strobilus, a slave

Lyconides, a young man

Phaedria, a girl

Flute-girls

---

[1] Spirit of the Hearth (*Lar familiaris*, guardian deity) of the house of Euclio; Euclio, an old miser; Staphyla, old housekeeper and slave of Euclio; Eunomia, sister of Megadorus; Megadorus, a wealthy old man; Pythodicus, slave of Megadorus; Congrio and Anthrax, cooks; Strobilus, slave of Lyconides; Lyconides, son of Eunomia; Phaedria, daughter of Euclio; Eleusium and Phrygia, flute-girls.

The Pot of Gold

Scene: Athens; the houses of Euclio and Megadorus face on to the street. There is a shrine with an altar to the side of Euclio's House.

PROLOGUE

Spoken by the Spirit of the Hearth, *who enters from Euclio's house.*

Welcome, audience…..

Firstly, I need to explain who I am. I am a spirit: my image stands by the hearth of this house here (*indicating Euclio's house*) from which you saw me come, and I take it upon myself to watch over and guard the house and family who live here.

I have possessed this house for many years now and I looked after it for the father and grandfather of the present owner.

The grandfather, when he was alive, secretly entrusted to me a hoard of gold, which he buried in a pot under the hearth itself; and he offered prayers to me to keep it safe for him.

When he was dying, he was so miserly that he did not, even then, want to tell his son about the treasure.

He preferred to leave him poorly off rather than to show him the gold's hiding-place.

On his death, he left his son a smallholding whereby, with hard work, he could eke out a miserable existence.

I then began to watch whether the son would hold me in any greater honour than his father had done. In the event, his attentions to me grew less and less and honours became fewer. I, in turn, gave him the attention he deserved and, in turn, he died in ignorance of the gold.

The grandson now lives here, and he has the same character as his father and grandfather.

But he has an only daughter; and she, every day, prays to me, burns incense, pours libations of wine, makes me garlands or gives me some other offering. It was out of consideration for her, that I ensured that her father, Euclio, discovered the treasure, so that he would be able to provide a dowry for her and so more easily find her a husband.

Unfortunately the daughter is now pregnant, having befriended a young man of excellent family during the festival celebrations of the Goddess Ceres. Whilst the young man knows her and who she is, she knows little of him: and her father knows nothing of the matter at all.

Today, I shall engineer matters in such a way that the old man who lives next door, Megadorus, will ask for the daughter's hand in marriage. My aim is to give the young man in this affair a greater opportunity to marry the daughter himself. Megadorus, the old man, is in fact the young man's uncle.

(A *noise from Euclio's house – of Euclio shouting – can suddenly be heard*)

That's Euclio shouting as usual. He's kicking his elderly housekeeper out of doors. He's wanting to check that his gold has not been stolen and, since he doesn't want her to know about it, he wants her out of the way first.

(*Exit* Spirit of the Hearth *into Euclio's house*)

ACT 1

(*Enter* Staphyla *from Euclio's house, followed by* Euclio, *who is pushing her*)

EUCLIO Get out! Get out! By Hercules, I want you out of my house! There's nothing for your prying eyes in here!

STAPHYLA What are you pushing me about for – an old woman like me?

EUCLIO Old women like you need pushing about!

STAPHYLA But why are you throwing me out of the house?

EUCLIO I'll tell you why, you useless object! Move over there, away from the door!

Look how she creeps along!

You'll soon see what I have in store for you! By Hercules, if I had a stick in my hand, you'd get a move on. What do you think you are – a tortoise?

STAPHYLA If the gods made me hang myself, I'd be no worse off than slaving in your house like this.

EUCLIO Now the wretched woman's talking to herself.

Listen, you! I'll gouge your eyes out before I let you pry into my affairs inside here!

Clear off! Go on! Stand over there! (*she complies*)

By Hercules, if you move one finger's-breadth from that spot, or turn round before I tell you, you will regret it!

(*aside*) One thing is certain – I've never seen a more vile old woman than her. In reality, I'm afraid of her – at least, I'm afraid of her catching me out when I'm off my guard and discovering where I've hidden my gold. She has eyes in the back of her head – that disagreeable woman! And I'm trying to make sure

24

my gold is still where I buried it – a matter which causes me great concern.

(*Exit* Euclio *into his house*)

STAPHYLA Well! I can't give any explanation as to what ails my master other than insanity. He pushes me out of the house, in exactly this fashion, as often as ten times a day. I don't know what's wrong with him: he never sleeps during the night and then sits about the house all day. He has such little desire to walk out of the house, you'd think he were lame.

Nor can I think of any way to hide his daughter's predicament from him: she's about to give birth any day!

Perhaps I should just put my head in a noose and have done with it!

[1.2]
(*Enter* Euclio *from his house*)

EUCLIO Good! I've checked that everything inside is safe and I can come outside now having put my mind at ease.

(*to Staphyla*) Go back inside and keep watch in there.
STAPHYLA Whatever next? I'm to keep watch inside!

Why? Is someone going to steal the house?

There's nothing else for thieves to take: the place is empty, apart from the cobwebs.
EUCLIO Yes, well, unfortunately Jupiter didn't make me quite as wealthy as King Philip or King Darius – not even to suit you, you old hag.

Anyway, I want those cobwebs kept watch over.

I'm poor. I admit it; and I have to put up with it. That's how the gods have made me.

Go inside and lock the door. I'll be back soon.

Make sure you don't let anyone into the house.

I want our fire to be put out, so that no-one is tempted to come asking for a light. If I find that fire alight, I'll extinguish you!

Say our water has run out, if anyone comes asking for any.

If anyone asks for a knife, or an axe, or a bowl, or any of the other things which neighbours have a habit of asking for, say burglars have broken in and taken everything.

Is that clear? I want no-one let into my house whilst I'm not here. In fact, if the Goddess of Good Fortune herself were to walk by, don't let her in.

STAPHYLA She wouldn't want to come in, even if she did walk by. She never has in the past.

EUCLIO That's enough! Now go inside.

STAPHYLA I've had enough and I'm going inside.

EUCLIO Make sure you lock the door: fasten both bolts. I'll be back soon.

(*Exit* Staphyla *into Euclio's house*)

EUCLIO I'm driven to distraction at the thought of having to leave my house. By Hercules, I'd rather not leave it, but I must. I have a tax refund to collect and if I don't ask for it, everyone will begin to suspect that I have gold at home. After all, it's not very likely that a man who is poor will not make the effort to go and collect his tax refund.

But even though I do all I can to prevent anyone from knowing, everyone seems to know. They all greet me

with greater kindness than they used to. They all
come up to me; they stop me to shake hands; they ask
me if I'm well and how I'm doing and whether
everything's all right.

Anyway, I'll get this job out of the way and then I'll
come home again as soon as ever I can.

(*Exit* Euclio *along the street*)

ACT 2

(*Enter* Eunomia *and* Megadorus *from Megadorus' house*)

EUNOMIA   I would hope, brother, that you would
appreciate that when I broach your affairs with you, I
have only your best interests at heart – as a sister
should.

Now, I am not deceived into thinking that you
consider us women anything but a nuisance. It's true
that we women are never short of words: 'a woman's
talk is never done', as they say.

But do remember this one thing, Megadorus: that we
are so close to each other. And when one of us sees
something clearly in the best interests of the other, it
is only right that we each point it out and offer our
advice. It would be quite wrong to remain silent out
of fear of speaking out. No; we must share our
thoughts with each other.

That is why I have brought you out here: so that I can
have a private word with you on a delicate matter
concerning yourself.

MEGADORUS   You are the finest of women! Give me your
hand.

EUNOMIA   (*looking around*) Who on earth are you talking
to?

MEGADORUS   You.

EUNOMIA   That's not how you usually speak to me.

MEGADORUS   Are you denying you are the finest of
women?

EUNOMIA   You really must speak the truth. There isn't a
finest woman: it is more a case, brother, that some
women are just worse than others.

MEGADORUS   My thoughts entirely: I would never disagree with you on that point, Eunomia.

EUNOMIA Now, listen to me.

MEGADORUS I wouldn't dare do anything else: I am at your command.

EUNOMIA   Good; I have come here to give you some sound advice.

MEGADORUS Of course you have.

EUNOMIA I have.

MEGADORUS What is it then, sister?

EUNOMIA A matter of your continued well-being.
       You should have children – may the gods grant that you do so – and with a view to this, I want you to take a wife.

MEGADORUS A death sentence!

EUNOMIA What was that?

MEGADORUS   Your words are addling my brains. You might as well pelt me with stones as speak like that.

EUNOMIA You must do as your sister tells you.

MEGADORUS If that's what you tell me to do, I'll do it!

EUNOMIA It's for the best.

MEGADORUS   What is? – a speedy death before the wedding? Alternatively, I would marry tomorrow if I thought my wife's funeral would be the day after.
       All right! I give in! Organise the wedding!

EUNOMIA I can obtain a very large dowry, Megadorus.
       The lady I have in mind was, shall we say, born some time ago. She is a lady of middle years.
       If you tell me to approach her with a proposal, I will do so.

MEGADORUS   You don't mind if I put some questions first?

EUNOMIA What would you like to know?

MEGADORUS The lady you have in mind is clearly of advancing years. Should she, together with an old man like me, by some happy stroke of good fortune, manage to produce a child, that child would reach adulthood, an only child with only dim memories of its parents.

I think on the whole I might as well save you the trouble. I can thank the gods that I was born into a sufficiently wealthy family. I have enough for my needs.

I am happy avoiding women of high status, rich dowries, loud authority, ivory-inlaid coaches and dresses of expensive purple cloth. Why should I become a slave to their extravagance?

EUNOMIA Well in that case, tell me whom you'd like to marry?

MEGADORUS I'll tell you what I do have in mind. Do you know Euclio, that rather poor old fellow who lives next door?

EUNOMIA Yes, he seems a very decent man.

MEGADORUS He has a young daughter. (*attempting not to sound too eager*) I wouldn't mind being engaged to her.

Now I know what you're going to say: she's poor. Well I can put up with that.

EUNOMIA May the gods bring you success!

MEGADORUS I do hope so.

EUNOMIA What do you want me to do now?

MEGADORUS Look after yourself.

EUNOMIA And you, brother.

(*Exit* Eunomia *along the street*)

MEGADORUS I'd better have a word with Euclio, if he's at
    home.
(*Megadorus sees Euclio coming along the street*)
    Ah, but here he is coming home from somewhere or
    other.

[2.2]
(*Enter* Euclio)

EUCLIO I had a feeling I'd be wasting my time, going out
    when I did. I didn't want to go in the first place. And
    there was no-one to pay my tax refund when I got
    there; in fact there was no-one about at all.
    And now, I'm hurrying home as quickly as I can. I've
    been out, but my mind's been at home all the time.
MEGADORUS Good morning, Euclio; I hope you are well!
EUCLIO Good morning, Megadorus.
MEGADORUS How are you? I hope everything's going
    well and as you would wish.
EUCLIO (*aside*) It's no accident when a rich man greets a
    poor one with cordiality. This man obviously knows
    that I have my gold; and that's why he's being so
    friendly.
MEGADORUS Did you say you're well?
EUCLIO I didn't say I was well off!
MEGADORUS Provided you are contented in your mind,
    then you have all you need to lead a happy life.
EUCLIO (*aside*) By Hercules, that old woman has told him
    about the gold. When I get in that house, I'll cut her
    tongue out and gouge out he eyes!
MEGADORUS You appear to be talking to yourself,
    Euclio.
EUCLIO I was complaining to myself of my poverty.

I have a grown-up girl, for whom I can provide no dowry. I don't know what to do with her; and I can't find a husband for her.

MEGADORUS Don't worry about that, Euclio: she'll be married. In fact, I'll give you a helping hand.

Now, tell me if you need anything.

EUCLIO (*aside*) He wants to give with one hand and take with the other. His eyes are greedy for my gold! He proffers me bread while hiding a knife behind his back. I do not trust the wealthy when they talk in friendly fashion to the poor. They shake your hand, then charge you for the privilege. They remind me of a giant squid: whatever they touch, they stick to – and squeeze dry.

MEGADORUS Could you spare me a moment, Euclio? I would like to have a quick word on a matter which concerns our mutual interest.

EUCLIO Oh no! I'm done for! My gold has been seized! And now this man, I'm sure, wants to negotiate a ransom. I'd better go in and check.

(*Euclio goes to the door of his house*)

MEGADORUS Where are you going?

EUCLIO I'll be back in a moment. There's something I just need to check indoors.

(*Exit* Euclio *into his house*)

MEGADORUS Oh dear; I suppose when I mention marrying his daughter, he'll think I'm making fun of him. He really does let his poverty get on top of him.

(*Enter* Euclio *from his house*)

EUCLIO May the gods be praised: it's safe! Yes it's quite
safe – (*suddenly doubtful*) unless some of it's
missing.

No; I'm being too fearful. When I went into the
house I was over-wrought.

But I'm back now, Megadorus: so what were you
saying?

MEGADORUS Well, I'm pleased you've recovered.

Now, I do have some questions, which I hope you
won't mind answering.

EUCLIO Provided they're questions which I'm happy to
answer.

MEGADORUS Tell me: what do you think of my family
background?

EUCLIO (*bemused and cautious throughout*) It's good.

MEGADORUS Would you agree I'm a man of my word?

EUCLIO Yes.

MEGADORUS Would you say I'm a man of propriety?

EUCLIO I've heard nothing bad of you.

MEGADORUS Do you know my age?

EUCLIO I know your age is substantial, (*aside*) like your
wealth.

MEGADORUS By Jupiter, I've always thought you to be a
fine upstanding citizen and I am now confirmed in
that opinion.

EUCLIO (*aside*) He has the scent of my gold.

(*to Megadorus*) What is your point?

MEGADORUS Now that we understand each other, and
since we want everything to turn out well for you and
myself – and your daughter – I wish to ask the hand
of your daughter in marriage. Do please give your
permission.

EUCLIO What!! Megadorus! This is disgraceful! Why do
you mock me? I am poor and I have never done you

any harm or anyone connected with you. I simply do not deserve this kind of treatment from you.

MEGADORUS By the gods, I haven't come out here to mock you or deride you in any way. I wouldn't do such a thing.

EUCLIO Then why are you asking to marry my daughter?

MEGADORUS Because I believe it will make each of us happier.

EUCLIO But, Megadorus, the thought occurs to me that you are a man of wealth and position, whereas I am the poorest of the poor. Now, if I have my daughter married to you, the thought occurs to me that I wouldn't be able to pull my share of the load. I'd be like an ass yoked alongside an ox: the ass would be soon exhausted and fall by the wayside. The ox wouldn't even notice: the ass might as well never have been born. The ass would be outclassed by the ox and would be the laughing stock of his fellow asses.

And if you and my daughter were to divorce, neither the wealthy nor the poor would have anything to do with me: I've as much chance of being accepted into your circles as an ass has of being accepted as an ox.

MEGADORUS I can assure you, you can only benefit from association with the upper echelons.

Listen to me: accept my proposal: promise her to me.

EUCLIO But I've nothing to give as a dowry.

MEGADORUS Don't worry about a dowry.

Her being betrothed as a pure young girl is dowry enough.

EUCLIO I simply did not want you to think I have some hidden treasure!

MEGADORUS Not at all! Now, promise her to me.

EUCLIO I agree.

(*A noise of digging is heard*)

EUCLIO   By Jupiter, what's that noise? Is there a thief about?

MEGADORUS What's wrong?

EUCLIO I thought I heard the sound of metal.

(*Exit* Euclio *into his house*)

MEGADORUS Oh, I did order for my garden to be dug over.

(*noticing Euclio's absence*) But where is the man? He seems to have gone. I've upset him by showing I want his friendship. It's human nature: whenever a rich man tries to win favour with a poor man, the poor man will be afraid to accept whatever is on offer; he becomes his own worst enemy. But, of course, he will only realise that when it's too late.

(*Enter* Euclio *from his house*)

EUCLIO (*to Staphyla within*) By Hercules, you useless old woman, if I don't have your tongue torn out by the roots, then I deserve a good flogging!

MEGADORUS By Hercules, Euclio! I see that you think I am the kind of person whose advancing years you can make fun of. That is unfair.

EUCLIO Not at all, Megadorus. I'm not in a position to, even if I wanted.

MEGADORUS So then: will you betroth your daughter to me?

EUCLIO Yes, but on condition that her dowry is as I said.

MEGADORUS So you agree?

EUCLIO Agreed.

(*Euclio and Megadorus shake hands*)

35

MEGADORUS May the Gods let it turn out well!

EUCLIO May they indeed, yes! But remember our agreement that my daughter comes without a dowry.

MEGADORUS Yes; that's agreed.

EUCLIO Now, I know you wealthy types don't always deal in a straightforward way. Firm agreements are found to have loopholes; and what's not been agreed is found to be binding – all in you favour!

MEGADORUS There's nothing contentious here.
Now, about the wedding – is there anything preventing us from holding it today?

EUCLIO Nothing at all! What a good idea!

MEGADORUS In that case, I'll go make the arrangements. Is there anything else we need to consider?

EUCLIO No, not at all.

MEGADORUS (*to slaves within his house*) Pythodicus! Come with me to the meat-market!

(*Enter* Pythodicus *from Megadorus' house; then Exeunt* Megadorus *and* Pythodicus *together down the street*)

EUCLIO He's gone. By the immortal Gods, that's the power of money! He's on the scent of my gold and he's not going to be sidetracked!
(*to Staphyla within his house*) Staphyla, where are you?! Why did you go blabbing to all the neighbours that I would give a dowry with my daughter? Staphyla! Can you hear me calling for you?

[2.3]
(*Enter* Staphyla *from Euclio's house*)

EUCLIO Now, hurry up and get the washing done. My daughter is betrothed; and it's today that I'm giving

36

her to Megadorus in marriage!

STAPHYLA May the Gods let it turn out well!

(*realising Phaedria's predicament*) But it can't be done!

This is all too sudden!

EUCLIO Just go inside and get on with your work; and make sure everything's ready by the time I return from some business I have to attend to!

And keep the doors locked! I'll be back soon.

(*Exit* Euclio *down the street*)

STAPHYLA What am I going to do now?! This could spell disaster for me and my young mistress!

She's about to give birth any day now and her disgrace will be public knowledge. We've managed to keep it all secret up till now; but that's not going to be possible any longer!

I'd better go inside now and make sure I get all the work my master gave me done before he comes home.

But I have a strong feeling there's trouble in store!

(*Exit* Staphyla *into Euclio's house*)

[2.4]

(*Enter from along the street* Pythodicus *with* Anthrax *and* Congrio, *who carry food from the market, including two lambs - one meaty and one much thinner, and with* Eleusium, *a beautiful flute-girl, and* Phrygia, *a fat flute-girl* [*played by a male actor in the style of a pantomime dame*])

PYTHODICUS After my master had bought all the food and hired you cooks and flute-girls in town, he

37

instructed me to divide everything into two parts.

ANTHRAX You're not dividing me into two parts, that's for sure! I'll work wherever you want – but in one piece!

CONGRIO What a fool! (*to Anthrax*) I'm sure there's nothing to get cut up about!

PYTHODICUS Of course, I'm not dividing you personally into two parts, Anthrax. The point is, my master is preparing for his wedding.

ANTHRAX Who's he marrying?

PYTHODICUS He's marrying the daughter of his next door neighbour, old Euclio.
And he wants half the food, one of you cooks, and one of you flute-girls here (*indicating Euclio's house*) and the rest of the food with a cook and a flute-girl in his own house, here. (*indicating Megadorus' house*)

ANTHRAX So, half here, half there? (*indicating as Pythodicus*)

PYTHODICUS Exactly so.

ANTHRAX What? Hasn't Euclio been able to pay anything towards his own daughter's wedding?

PYTHODICUS Not much chance of that!

ANTHRAX What's the problem?

PYTHODICUS You ask what's the problem? Try getting blood out of a stone!

ANTHRAX He's as bad as that?

PYTHODICUS He certainly is. I wouldn't say he's tight-fisted, but: he'll swear by Gods and men that he's been reduced to penury simply because the smoke from his miserly fire is escaping from his house. He's so concerned about losing anything that he only breathes out with great reluctance.

ANTHRAX Really?

PYTHODICUS Yes, really.

> And when he takes a bath, he's in tears when he comes to throw the water away.

ANTHRAX Since I'm a slave, do you think it would be worth asking him to give me some money to buy my freedom with?

PYTHODICUS He wouldn't give you the time of day.

> The last time he went to the barber's to have his nails cut, he picked up the clippings and took them home.

ANTHRAX No, I wouldn't say he was tight-fisted either.

PYTHODICUS Anyway, we've no time for tales about old Euclio.

> Now tell me, which of you is the quicker?

ANTHRAX I am; I'm much the better altogether.

PYTHODICUS I'm talking about cooking not stealing.

ANTHRAX I'm talking about cooking.

PYTHODICUS (to Congrio) What do you say?

CONGRIO I am as I appear.

ANTHRAX Him?! He's a seven-day wonder: it takes him seven days to cook anything!

CONGRIO At least I cook the food, not steal it!

ANTHRAX Hey! We'll have less of that!

(*Anthrax and Congrio square up to each other*)
[2.5]
PYTHODICUS (*intervening*) All right; that's enough!

> (*to Anthrax*) Now you, take that lamb there – the fattest one – and bring it into our house here. (*indicating Megadorus' house*)

ANTHRAX (*seizing the fatter lamb*) Right you are!

(*Exit* Anthrax *into Megadorus' house, with some of the food and the lamb*)

PYTHODICUS And you, Congrio, take the rest of the food and that other lamb into that house there. (*indicating Euclio's house*)

CONGRIO Hey! That's not the way to divide the food up: they've got the fat lamb!

PYTHODICUS Don't worry – you're having the fat flute-girl! (*indicating Phrygia, who looks approvingly at Congrio*)
(*to Phrygia*) Phrygia, you keep with him.
(*so Phrygia stands by Congrio*)

PYTHODICUS (*to Eleusium*) And you, Eleusium, come in here with us. (*indicating Megadorus' house*)

(*Exit* Eleusium *into Megadorus' house*)

CONGRIO You're a sly one, Pythodicus – sending me off to work for that old miser! If I want anything, I'll have to shout myself hoarse before I'll get it.

PYTHODICUS You ungrateful fool! I do you a favour and all you do is complain

CONGRIO How's that?

PYTHODICUS How's that?! Well, to begin with, there won't be a crowd of people in there to deal with. And if you need anything, bring it from home so that you won't have to trouble asking for it.
We, on the other hand, have to cope with a huge crowd of guests and a houseful of slaves. Then there's all the fancy ornaments, jewellery, fine clothes and silver dinner services: and if anything goes missing (and I realise you won't steal anything - if nothing's put in your way) they'll say "The cooks have stolen it; seize 'em, tie 'em up, flog 'em, throw 'em in prison!"

40

But you won't have this problem. There's nothing there for you to steal. So come along

CONGRIO I'm coming.

[2.6]

PYTHODICUS (*to Staphyla within Euclio's house*) Staphyla! Come and open up the door!

STAPHYLA (*from within*) Who's that?

PYTHODICUS It's me, Pythodicus!

(*Enter* Staphyla *from Euclio's house*)

STAPHYLA What do you want?

PYTHODICUS I've a cook for you and a flute-girl and the food for the wedding. Megadorus told me to deliver them here.

STAPHYLA (*surveying the food*) I didn't realise Megadorus was teetotal.

PYTHODICUS He isn't.

STAPHYLA Where's the booze, then?

PYTHODICUS There'll be plenty, when Sir gets back from the market.

STAPHYLA We've no wood for the fires.

CONGRIO There'll be some beams.

STAPHYLA Beams?!

CONGRIO They're made of wood. That's all you need.

STAPHYLA What's that! I know you like starting fires, but this dinner and your pay are hardly reason for us to burn the house down!

CONGRIO I take it back!

PYTHODICUS Just take them all inside.

STAPHYLA Come this way.

41

[2.7]
PYTHODICUS Make sure you take care.

(*Exeunt* Staphyla, Congrio, *with the thin lamb and the food, and* Phrygia *into Euclio's house, leaving the door open*)

PYTHODICUS I'd better see what the cooks are doing here.
(*indicating Megadorus' house*) I've got my work cut out, looking after that lot! I wouldn't put it past them to eat all the food themselves! Anyway, there's no point in standing about here talking to myself as if there's no work to be done – and the house full of those robbers!

(*Exit* Pythodicus *into Megadorus' house*)

[2.8]
(*Enter* Euclio *from along the street, carrying a small package and two or three bedraggled flowers*)

EUCLIO Now I wanted to make sure that I'd made handsome provision for my daughter's wedding! So I went to the market to ask the price of fish. They said it was dear. Lamb was dear; beef, veal, seafood, pork were dear.
Everything was dear! Far too dear for my purse! So I'm now in a bad temper having found nothing to buy! What a rabble they were at the market!
Then, as I was walking home, I began to think. "Waste not, want not" I said to myself. No point throwing money away on the wedding – better to be careful. But would my profligate heart rule my accountant's head? No. My heart agreed with me,

that I should spend as little as possible on my daughter's wedding.

So now, I've bought a little incense (*indicating his package*) and these few flowers. These will be placed on our hearth and dedicated to the Spirit who lives there, so that he may bless my daughter's marriage.

But what's this?! The house doors are open: and there's something going on inside. Don't say we're being robbed!

CONGRIO (*in the doorway, to someone within*) Go get a bigger pot, if you can, from a neighbour. This one's too small – it won't hold everything.

EUCLIO A pot! By Hercules, my gold's being stolen: someone's looking for my pot!

Apollo, I beg you, come and help me. Shoot down these gold-robbers with your arrows! Help me, if you've ever helped anyone!

But I'd better go in quickly, before I'm completely ruined!

(*Exit* Euclio *into his house*)

[2.9]
(*Enter* Anthrax *into doorway of Megadorus' house*)

ANTHRAX (*to slaves within*) Dromo, scale these fish! Machaerio, fillet the eel and those fish over there as fast as you can! I'm going next door to borrow a bread-pan from Congrio. You, I want that chicken plucked.

(*Sounds of a commotion come from Euclio's house*)

ANTHRAX But what's that din coming from next door?

43

It's probably just the cooks getting the food ready. Perhaps I'd better go back in here – I don't want that kind of row going on here as well!

(*Exit* Anthrax *into Megadorus' house*)

ACT 3

(*Enter* Congrio *and* Phrygia *in a state of alarm, from Euclio's house*)

CONGRIO Help! Get out of my way, everyone; I've got to get away from here! This is the first time I've had to cook for Bacchanalian revels! I didn't realise being beaten was part of the job!
That was painful – and the old man's waving his cane about as if it's part of his daily exercise routine!

(*Enter* Euclio *into his doorway, cane in hand*)

CONGRIO Oh no! I'm done for! They're coming outside: it's him! He's following me!

(*Congrio withdraws into a recess; Phrygia, in alarm, also hides.*)

CONGRIO I'll hide here. I've learnt my lesson: I've never seen anyone wield a cane more stylishly!
He certainly drove me outside without any difficulty!
[3.2]
EUCLIO Come back! Where are you going? (*sees Congrio*) Get hold of him!
CONGRIO All right! What are you shouting for?
EUCLIO You should be brought before the magistrates!
CONGRIO What for?
EUCLIO For carrying a knife.
CONGRIO Cooks do carry knives!
EUCLIO Then why did you threaten me?
CONGRIO (*aside*) I'm beginning to think I should have stabbed him when I had the chance!

EUCLIO   You're the most dangerous criminal at large today; and there's no-one I'd rather see given a good beating!

CONGRIO   That's obvious enough! Your actions speak for themselves. And thanks to that cane of yours, my back's more tender than one of my finest steaks. But what were you setting about me for, anyway, you worthless beggar?

EUCLIO   What for?! You've the cheek to ask that?!
Perhaps I didn't hit you hard enough!

CONGRIO   Keep off, by Hercules, or you'll regret it: I'm nobody's fool, you know!

EUCLIO   Nobody's fool! You'll just be nobody, when I've finished with you!
So what business did you have to be in my house when I was away? You weren't there on instructions of mine, were you? So come on, what were you doing?

CONGRIO   Don't get so excited! I came to cook for the wedding.

EUCLIO   What's it got to do with you, then, whether I eat my food cooked or raw? Is it your job to watch over me?

CONGRIO   I'd just like to know: do you want me to cook for you or don't you?

EUCLIO   And I'd just like to know: with you here, will my possessions be safe in my own home?

CONGRIO   I can assure you: I'll be quite happy, if I succeed in taking safely away from here what I brought. I've no desire for anything of yours.

EUCLIO   (*sarcastically*) Oh no; of course not;
(*pointedly*) I understand entirely.

CONGRIO   Why exactly is it that you don't want me to cook for you? What have I done? What have I said that you've taken offence at?

EUCLIO   Ah, that's a fine question from a man who's searched every nook and cranny of my home!

Now, if you'd kept to your oven, which is where cooks are supposed to be, you wouldn't have had your head cracked! Don't say you didn't deserve it!

And in case you are in any doubt, I wish to make it entirely clear that if you so much as approach my door, unless I tell you to, you will regret it for the rest of your days. Do you understand?!

(*Exit* Euclio *into his house*)

CONGRIO   (*to Euclio, as he enters his house*) Where are you going? Come back! By Laverna, Goddess of thieves, unless you order my pots and pans to be returned to me, I'll make sure everybody knows you for the villain you are!

(*aside*) Now what am I going to do? This clearly is not my day. I'm only being paid a few drachmas for this job, and I'll spend more than that on medical bills!

[3.3]
(*Enter* Euclio, *concealing the pot of gold under his cloak*)

EUCLIO   (*revealing the pot of gold to the audience*)
This, by Hercules, will go wherever I go. I'm keeping it with me. And I'm not running the risk of leaving it in there (*indicating his house*).

Now, please, everyone – cooks, flute girls – go inside as you please. And take with you your crowd of

47

cheap slaves, if you want. Cook, work, beaver away now to your hearts' content!

CONGRIO Oh, everything's fine, now that you've cracked my skull open!

EUCLIO Go inside! You're here to cook, not make speeches.

CONGRIO Listen, old man. I want some compensation for that beating you gave me. I'm here to cook, not to be beaten.

EUCLIO (*sarcastically*) Going to take me to court, are you? Don't be a nuisance: go and cook the dinner – or clear off, away from my house!

CONGRIO Get out of my way – please.

(*Exeunt* Congrio *and* Phrygia *into Euclio's house*)

[3.4]

EUCLIO He's gone.

By the immortal gods, it's a bold venture a poor man undertakes when he does business with a wealthy one! And now, I have Megadorus taking advantage of me, a poor man, in every way he can. He pretends he sent the cooks round to my house to help me. He sent them for one reason only: to steal this (*indicating the pot of gold*) from a miserable old man like me. And of course, it had to be that dunghill-cockerel in there, that used to belong to the old woman, which very nearly caused my downfall. It began to scratch about with its claws at the precise spot where this (*indicating the pot*) was buried. I needn't tell you how alarmed I became: I picked up a stick - knocked the cock's head off – the thief! Caught in the act! It wouldn't surprise me if those cooks hadn't offered that cock a reward for revealing the hiding-place. Good job I stopped them in their tracks!

(*looking down the street*) But look; here comes Megadorus, my future son-in-law, back from town. I can't really just let him walk past: I'd better have a word with him.

[3.5]
(*Enter* Megadorus *along the street*)

MEGADORUS (*aside*) I have explained my plans for this marriage to many of my friends. For Euclio's daughter, they only have praise and approve the wisdom of my course of action.

Now, it is my opinion that if all the better off people did the same, and married the dowerless daughters of the less well off, our city would enjoy much greater harmony, men would begrudge our wealth much less, our wives would treat us with far greater respect and we would find our household bills considerably reduced. Such an approach is tailor-made for the vast majority of our citizens.

Now, I may encounter disagreement from those whose greed and insatiableness defy all measurement. They put forward arguments such as "Whom will the wealthy young women with dowries marry, if the poor girls take all the husbands?" The answer, of course is that they can marry whoever they want, provided no dowry accompanies them! And I am sure that, instead of a dowry, they would bring a much better attitude to their marriages! They would soon forget those fancy mules they like to draw their carriages. Mules cost more than horses now – but they'd be cheaper than old Gallic geldings by the time I'd finished!

EUCLIO (*aside*) The gods must love me: his words are music to my ears – a beautiful speech from a man of thrift!

MEGADORUS We don't want any woman ever to be able to say to her husband "Well now, the dowry I brought you was far greater than the money you had before, and so it's entirely fair that I should be given fine clothes and gold, serving girls, mules, drivers, attendants, boys and my own carriages".

EUCLIO He obviously understands the ways of married ladies. If only we could have him appointed Minister for Women!

MEGADORUS A tradesman has his cart, and nowadays, wherever you go, you see more carts round a town house than ever you see at a farm.

The real problem, of course, is that these tradesmen want paying! You're confronted by the fuller, the dress-maker, the jeweller, the wool-worker. Then there are the embroiderers, the underwear-makers, the bridal veil makers, the dyers of purple cloth and the dyers of yellow cloth; with them come the sleeve-makers, the balsam-scented footwear makers, the linen salesmen and the shoe-makers; closely followed by the squatting cobblers, the slipper-makers and the sandal-manufacturers. Standing by them are the mallow-dyers and the belt-makers.

Just when you think you've got them paid, along come a dozen more with their bills: they stand like warders in your hall – weavers, fringe-makers, jewel-box makers. You settle their accounts and when you think you've finally rid yourself of them all, along come the saffron-dyers or some other nuisances: there's always somebody who wants paying!

EUCLIO I'd go up to him, were it not that I might interrupt his flow. He certainly understands female extravagance: I'll let him go on!

MEGADORUS When finally you've dealt with all these triviality-merchants, you're then approached by a soldier with a tax-demand – for money for the army. By this time, you have to go and talk to your bank! The soldier has to miss his lunch, waiting for your tax money. You then discover that you're overdrawn at the bank, and the soldier has to be told to come back another day!

Yes, large dowries bring their own disadvantages and intolerable female prodigality!

But the girl who has no dowry – she can be controlled by her husband! Much better than the havoc wrought by a dowry!

But I see my neighbour by my door. Euclio, how are you?

EUCLIO All the better for listening to your speech.

[3.6]

MEGADORUS You heard what I said?

EUCLIO Every word from the beginning.

MEGADORUS (*regarding Euclio critically*) Now Euclio – how can I put this? – I think perhaps you might smarten up a little for your daughter's wedding.

EUCLIO Those who put on airs and graces without the wealth to support it, should remember their station in life. By the Gods, Megadorus, I'm like all poor people: I've no secret wealth stashed away at home!

MEGADORUS Come now! You've enough for yourself.

51

And may the Gods increase your prosperity – and keep safe what you have!

EUCLIO (*aside, looking surreptitiously at his pot of gold*) I don't like that phrase "what you have".

He knows as well as I do what I have here. That old woman must have told him!

MEGADORUS   Are you holding a meeting over there, Euclio?

EUCLIO I am simply preparing my complaint against you, Megadorus, and with good reason!

MEGADORUS What complaint?

EUCLIO "What complaint?" did you say? I am a poor man, and you have filled every corner of my house with thieves. You have sent cooks into my house, each with six hands to steal with: I couldn't watch them all even if I had eyes in the back of my head! And as for that flute-girl, if the fountain of Pirene[1] ran with wine, she'd drink it dry all by herself! And then, as for the food....

MEGADORUS   What's wrong with the food? There's enough for an army. And I sent you a lamb as well.

EUCLIO   A lamb?! I've never seen such a scrawny specimen!

MEGADORUS Scrawny?! How can you say that?

EUCLIO Because it's all skin and bone. It looks all care-worn. It's so thin that, with the sun behind it, you'd be able to see through it!

MEGADORUS Just a minute; I bought that lamb myself.

EUCLIO Well, you're the man to bury it then; for I think it's dead!

---

[1] A fountain in Corinth.

MEGADORUS We need to have a drink together today, Euclio.

EUCLIO But I don't drink, thank you.

MEGADORUS But I'm having a jar of vintage wine sent across from my cellars.

EUCLIO No thank you. It is a rule of mine to drink only water.

MEGADORUS Oh come on! A drop of wine won't do you any harm!

EUCLIO (*aside*) I know his game! He'll ply me with wine and then "what I have" (*indicating the pot*) will disappear round to his house! I'll make sure it doesn't: I'll hide it somewhere out here. By the time I've finished, he'll have wasted his efforts and his wine!

MEGADORUS If you don't mind, I need to go and bathe and be ready to make sacrifice.

(*Exit* Megadorus *into his house*)

EUCLIO (*addressing the pot of gold*) By the Gods, my dear little pot, you have your enemies, as does the gold entrusted to you!
But here is the altar of the Goddess of Faith. And here, by Faith's altar, I shall hide you.
(*praying*) Goddess of Faith, you know me and I you. (*hides the pot behind the altar*) As I entrust this to you, remain true to your name. I come to you, Faith, relying on your faithfulness.

(*Exit* Euclio *into his house*)

ACT 4

(*Enter* Strobilus *from along the street*)

STROBILUS Virtuous slaves do as I do and do not consider their masters' orders a source of irritation or hardship. And the slave who desires to serve his master's wishes, must put his master first and himself second. If he sleeps, he must sleep in the knowledge that he is a slave. He should read his master's wishes in his expression and a four-horse chariot should not match the speed with which he carries out his master's orders. The slave who bears this in mind will not receive a tax demand payable in lashes and will not polish up his master's chains with his ankles. Now, my young master is in love with the daughter of poor Euclio. And my master has been told that she's to marry Megadorus, their next door neighbour. He's sent me to reconnoitre and report back. Now, I won't arouse any suspicion if I sit by this altar, (*sits beside the altar on the far side from Euclio's door*) and from here I can watch both houses' to-ings and fro'-ings.

[4.2]
(*Enter* Euclio *from his house*)

EUCLIO Goddess of Faith, please make sure you tell no-one my gold is here. I'm not afraid of anyone finding it: it's in a well-hidden place. By the Gods, it would be a fine prize for anyone who did find it – a pot full of gold!
(*Strobilus reacts on hearing this*)
Goddess of Faith, make sure no-one does!

54

Now I'm going to bathe, to prepare myself for making a sacrifice. I don't want to delay my neighbour from claiming my daughter in marriage and taking her home.

Make sure, Goddess of Faith, particularly at this time, that I can return to recover my pot of gold safe and sound. To your good faith, I have entrusted my gold: it's hidden in your shrine, by your altar.

(*Exit* Euclio *into his house*)

STROBILUS By the Immortal Gods! What a thing to overhear! He says he's hidden a pot full of gold here, inside this shrine of the Goddess of Faith.

Well, Goddess of Faith, there's no need to be more faithful to him than to me! And that man, if I'm not mistaken, is the father of the girl with whom my master is in love. Well, while he's otherwise engaged, I'll take a look round this shrine to see if I can find his gold.

(*Strobilus begins to look for the gold around the altar*)

If I find it, Goddess of Faith, I'll pour out a jarful of honeyed wine in your honour; and when I've done that, I'll drink it myself!

(*Enter* Euclio *from his house. Strobilus hides at the side of the altar*)

[4.3]

EUCLIO There must be a reason for that raven singing on my left-hand side. It was scratching at the earth with its claws, croaking all the time. Well, my heart's in my mouth: it's beating ten to the dozen. Anyway, I've got here quickly!

(Euclio *sees Strobilus hiding by the altar*)

[4.4]
EUCLIO   Come out here, you grovelling worm! You weren't in evidence before, but now you are, you're dead! By the Gods, I'll teach you a lesson! (*threatens Strobilus*)

STROBILUS   What are you threatening me for? What have I got to do with you, old man? Keep your hands to yourself!

EUCLIO   You deserve all you get! You're a thief! Are you denying it?! You're a thief aren't you?!

STROBILUS   What have I stolen from you, then?

EUCLIO   Give it me back!

STROBILUS   Give what back?

EUCLIO   Come on!

STROBILUS   I've taken nothing of yours.

EUCLIO   Whatever you have taken, give it me back! Come on!

STROBILUS   How do you mean "Come on"?

EUCLIO   You won't get away with it!

STROBILUS   Away with what?

EUCLIO   Put it down!

STROBILUS   I'll put it down to your needing your head examined!

EUCLIO   Just put it down. Don't try to be funny! This is no joke.

STROBILUS   Put what down? Perhaps if you were to put a name to it…
But, by Hercules, I haven't touched a thing. I certainly haven't taken anything.

EUCLIO Show me your hands!

STROBILUS (*holds out both hands*) There you are!

EUCLIO Right! Where's your third hand?!

STROBILUS (*aside*) The old man's mad! The spirits have got to him!

(*to Euclio, sarcastically*) You're being unfair on me, I think.

EUCLIO I am being completely unfair, in not having you hanged. And you will be, if you don't confess!

STROBILUS May the Gods destroy me, if I've stolen anything of yours.

I haven't stolen anything: (*aside*) even though it wasn't for the want of trying.

EUCLIO Come on, now: shake out your cloak.

STROBILUS (*obeying*) As you want.

EUCLIO Perhaps it's hidden under your tunic.

STROBILUS Feel anywhere you want!

EUCLIO Clever, aren't you? You'll soon have me think you didn't take anything! I know your tricks!

Come on; show me your right hand again.

STROBILUS (*obeying*) All right?

EUCLIO Now the left one.

STROBILUS (*obeying*) There you are: both of them.

EUCLIO All right; that's enough searching. Hand it over!

STROBILUS Hand what over?

EUCLIO Don't try to fool me. You know you've got it!

STROBILUS I've got it?!

Got what?

EUCLIO Ah! I'm not telling you that! I know you'd like to know.

Anyway, whatever it is, it's mine: so hand it over!

STROBILUS You're mad! You've searched me as you've wanted and you've found nothing on me.

EUCLIO (*believing he hears a noise by the altar*) Wait a
    moment! What was that? Was there someone else
    there with you?
    By Hercules, I'm ruined! There's someone else over
    there causing trouble; but if I let this one go,
    (*indicating Strobilus*) he'll be off with a clean pair of
    heels.
    On the other hand, I've searched him and he doesn't
    have anything; so (*to Strobilus*) you, clear off.
STROBILUS (*runs off further down the street away from
    the altar*) The curse of Jupiter and all the Gods on
    you!
EUCLIO What a charming fellow!
    I'm going to have a look around there and if I catch
    your accomplice, I'll string him up! Well, are you
    going or aren't you?
STROBILUS I'm going. (*moves away, but loiters by
    Megadorus' doorway*)
EUCLIO Make sure I don't see you again!

(*Euclio begins to search for the pot of gold by the altar, not
seeing that Strobilus is still in sight*)

[4.5]
STROBILUS (*aside*) I'd rather die a horrible death than
    miss the chance of trapping the old man.
    Now, he's not going to risk hiding his gold around
    here again. I suppose he'll bring it out with him and
    hide it somewhere else.
    Just a minute! Here comes the old man now and he's
    bringing the gold with him.
    I'll keep in this doorway for a while longer.

[4.6]

EUCLIO If the Goddess of Faith can't be faithful, who can?
Well, she's come within a hair's breadth of making a
real fool out of me! If it hadn't been for that raven,
I'd be completely ruined!

By Hercules, I'd like to meet that raven, so that I
could give him something for his help .....; well, give
him, that is, my thanks – we don't want to overdo it,
do we?

Now, I need to think of somewhere out of the way
where I can hide this (*indicating the pot of gold*).

I know: there's a grove sacred to Silvanus outside the
city walls. No-one goes there: it's all willow trees
and dense undergrowth. Silvanus might prove more
reliable than Goddess Faith.

(*Exit* Euclio *down the street*)

STROBILUS Yes!! The Gods are clearly intent on looking
after me!

Now, I'll easily reach that grove of Silvanus before
he does; and I'll find a tree to climb from where I can
watch where the old man buries his gold.

I know my master told me to wait here: but that pot
of gold is worth the risk!

(*Exit* Strobilus *down the street*)

[4.7]
(*Enter* Lyconides *and* Eunomia *from along the street*)

LYCONIDES   .....so that's what happened, mother: and
now you know the whole story about Euclio's

daughter.

And now I beg you, as I have begged you before, please discuss the matter with my uncle Megadorus.

EUNOMIA Now, you know that I will try to achieve what you want; and I'm pretty certain I can convince my brother. After all, you're being entirely open, if, as you say, you made her pregnant having got yourself drunk.

LYCONIDES Would I lie to your face, mother?

PHAEDRIA (*from within Euclio's house*) Nurse! Nurse!
The pains have started! Goddess Juno Lucina!
My trust is in you now!

LYCONIDES (*hearing Phaedria*) Mother, the deed speaks louder than my words! It's her! She's going to give birth!

EUNOMIA Why don't you come with me to visit your uncle, here? Then I am sure I'd be able to persuade him to accede to your request.

LYCONIDES You go; I'll follow you, mother.

(*Exit* Eunomia *into Megadorus' house*)

LYCONIDES (*aside*) I'm just wondering where my slave, Strobilus, is. I told him to wait here.
When I think about it, though, perhaps the job I gave him has taken him elsewhere – in which case it would be unfair to criticize him. I'll go inside: after all, behind these doors, my fate is being decided!

(*Exit* Lyconides *into Megadorus' house*)

[4.8]
(*Enter* Strobilus *along the road, carrying the pot of gold*)

STROBILUS   I remember stories of fabulous birds which
nest in golden mountains: well I am richer than they
are now. And as for all those kings – mere beggars. I
am King Philip himself.
This is my lucky day!
When I left here some time ago, I went straight to
that Grove of Silvanus – and got there before the old
man. In fact well before he had arrived, I'd hidden
myself in a tree from where I could see where he was
going to hide his gold. When he'd finished burying it,
I came back down from my tree and dug up his pot,
which is full of gold! But then I saw him coming
back to check his hiding place: but he didn't see me –
I managed to hide out of the way.
(*Looking down the street*) Ah! But here he comes
now. I'll go home and make sure this (*indicating the
pot*) is well hidden.

(*Exit* Strobilus *down the street in the opposite direction to
that in which he came*)

[4.9]
(*Enter* Euclio, *along the street, distressed*)

EUCLIO   I'm ruined! Dead! I've been robbed! Where
should I look?! Where should I not look?! I'd shout
"Stop thief" if I knew whom to stop!
I don't know what to think; my mind's a blank; I
stumble blindly I know not where! I don't know
where I am – or who I am! I can't think or see
straight at all.

(*to the audience*) Audience, I need your help: I need you to tell me the name of the person who took it!
(*after a pause*) You don't seem very forthcoming! Mind you, you look a villainous crew, yourselves!
Well, someone has it: but I don't know who! I'm ruined, completely done for! This is a sad day indeed, and it's brought me poverty and starvation.
I must be the most abject person in the whole wide world: what is life to me when I have lost the gold I have so carefully guarded? I have denied myself for so long: and now others are enjoying themselves at the expense of my ruin!
(*wailing uncontrollably*) This is unbearable!

(*Enter* Lyconides *from Megadorus' house*)

LYCONIDES Who on earth is making that wailing noise outside our house here?
Oh no! It's Euclio! I'm done for! It's all in the open! He's found out his daughter's had a baby!
The only question now is whether I should go or stay – whether I should approach him or clear off! I don't know what to do.

[4.10]
EUCLIO (*not seeing Lyconides*) Who's that talking there?
LYCONIDES It's me, I'm afraid: I'm in rather a sorry state, I know.
EUCLIO You're in a sorry state?! What about me? Look at the disaster I'm facing!
LYCONIDES Well, don't get too worked up about it.
EUCLIO How can I possibly not get worked up about it?
LYCONIDES Well – er – the matter which is the cause of your trouble....., well, I am the culprit – I admit it.

62

EUCLIO What's that?!

LYCONIDES I'm afraid it's true.

EUCLIO What have I done to deserve this, young man? What have I and my children done to deserve ruin at your hands?

LYCONIDES A god led me astray: a god put temptation in my path.

EUCLIO How was that?

LYCONIDES I know I've done wrong and I know I'm to blame: that's why I've come to you – to ask you to look at the matter reasonably and to forgive me.

EUCLIO But how could you dare interfere with what was not yours to interfere with?

LYCONIDES Well, what's done is done. I can't undo the past. It must have been the will of the gods: If it had not been their will, it wouldn't have happened; I'm sure of that.

EUCLIO And I believe it is the will of the gods that I should wring your neck!

LYCONIDES Please, think again!

EUCLIO Why did you take from me what was dearest to me?

LYCONIDES It was a case of too much wine and I was in love!

EUCLIO You impudent young man!…daring to come to me with that kind of talk! If we were to accept excuses like that, we would all be able to commit daylight robbery; and if we were caught, we'd be able to say "It's all right, we were drunk and in love!"

LYCONIDES Yes, and that's why I've come to you, voluntarily, to plead for forgiveness for my stupidity.

EUCLIO I'm not impressed by excuses for wrongdoing. You know you've taken my treasure.

LYCONIDES (*aside*) Indeed, she is a treasure!

(*to Euclio*) I admit it. And having taken "your treasure", I'd like to have "your treasure" for my own.

EUCLIO What's that you say!

LYCONIDES I'd like your agreement, of course; but I think we'd go very well together. I'm sure you'd come to realise that, Euclio.

EUCLIO By Hercules, I'll have you brought before the magistrates, unless you give me it back!

LYCONIDES Give you what back?

EUCLIO What you've stolen!

LYCONIDES Stolen?! What are you talking about?

EUCLIO Oh, so now, butter wouldn't melt in your mouth!

LYCONIDES You'll have to tell me what I'm supposed to have stolen.

EUCLIO My pot of gold! That's what I want back; and you've admitted to stealing it.

LYCONIDES By the Gods, I've admitted to no such thing! I haven't stolen anything!

EUCLIO You deny it?

LYCONIDES I certainly do. I know of no gold – or pots, for that matter.

EUCLIO Yes you do! You stole it from that Grove of Silvanus.

Now come on; give it me back! (*worriedly*) Or rather, I'll let you keep half. After all, even though you are a thief, I don't want to be a nuisance. So come on, bring it back.

LYCONIDES You're not making any sense in calling me a thief. I thought you had a bone to pick with me on quite a different matter.

There is an important matter, Euclio, which I need time to discuss with you. Could you spare me the time now?

EUCLIO Tell me truly: did you steal my gold?

LYCONIDES No I did not.

EUCLIO And you don't know who did steal it?

LYCONIDES No; I don't know that either.

EUCLIO And if you find out who took it, you'll tell me?

LYCONIDES Yes.

EUCLIO And you're not going to receive a share of the gold or meet up with the thief later?

LYCONIDES No.

EUCLIO What if you're cheating me?

LYCONIDES May Jupiter be my witness.

EUCLIO All right. Now, what do you want to talk to me about?

LYCONIDES Perhaps you do not know my family. Megadorus, who lives there, is my uncle. My father was Antimachus; I am called Lyconides and my mother is Eunomia.

EUCLIO I do know your family. Now, what is the matter you wish to discuss?

LYCONIDES You have a daughter.

EUCLIO Yes, she lives at home.

LYCONIDES I believe she is engaged to be married to my uncle, Megadorus.

EUCLIO That is correct.

LYCONIDES He has instructed me to tell you that he is breaking off the engagement.

EUCLIO Breaking off the engagement... with everything ready and the wedding ceremony all prepared?! May all the Gods and Goddesses on Mount Olympus destroy whoever it was that stole my gold and brought me to the brink of ruin!

LYCONIDES Don't worry: and don't say anything to offend the gods. With a little help from them, this should all turn out very well for you and your daughter.

Come on; say "May the Gods help us".

EUCLIO (*unimpressed*) May the Gods help us.

LYCONIDES And may the Gods help me!

Now listen!

However worthless a man may be in other respects, if he knows he's in the wrong, he'll feel ashamed and want to make amends.

Now if I have made a mistake and acted improperly towards you and your daughter, then I want you to forgive me..... and to give her to me as a wife..... which, in the circumstances, is what the law requires – of me.

I admit I did not treat your daughter as I should have done..... It was the wine – and youthful enthusiasm.....

EUCLIO (*wailing*) Oh no! What's this I hear!

LYCONIDES Why are you so upset? I've made you a grandfather and you are about to celebrate your daughter's marriage.

Yes, your daughter's had our baby and for this reason my uncle has broken off his engagement to her in my favour.

Go in, and you'll find it's as I say.

EUCLIO Disaster! In fact, I'm beset by one disaster after another!

I'd better go inside and find out the truth for myself.

(*Exit* Euclio *into his house*)

LYCONIDES (*to Euclio within*) I'll be with you in a moment.

(*aside*) A difficult time, but we're nearly home and dry!

(*looking around*) Now, my slave, Strobilus, doesn't seem to be where I told him to be. I'll wait here for him a little while and go in later. That'll give Euclio time to find out about his daughter from that old woman who's looked after her: she knows all about it.

(*Lyconides waits in the doorway of Euclio's house*)

ACT 5

(Lyconides *remains waiting in the doorway of Euclio's house. Enter* Strobilus *from along the street*)

STROBILUS   Ye immortal Gods! What magnificent blessings you have bestowed on me – in the form of a beautiful pot full to the brim with gold! Who is richer than I? Who, in the whole of Athens, has the Gods to help them as much as I?

LYCONIDES (*aside*) I can hear someone's voice.

STROBILUS (*aside, catching sight of Lyconides*) Is that my master there?

LYCONIDES (*aside*) Is that my slave?

STROBILUS (*aside*) It is my master.

LYCONIDES (*aside*) It is my slave.

STROBILUS (*aside*) I'd better go to meet him.

LYCONIDES (*aside*) I can have a word with him now. I suppose he's done as I ordered and spoken with the old woman who's looked after the girl.

STROBILUS (*aside*) Why not tell him I've found the gold? Then I could ask him to set me free from my slavery. Yes, I'll tell him all about it.
     (*to Lyconides as they meet*) Lyconides, I have found…

LYCONIDES Found what?

STROBILUS This isn't a childish riddle.

LYCONIDES That'd make a change. Anyway, now that you're here, I'd better go inside. (*starts to go into Euclio's house*)

STROBILUS Master! Wait a moment. I've something to say! Just listen, will you?

LYCONIDES All right. Say what you have to say.

STROBILUS Lyconides, I have today found untold riches!

LYCONIDES Oh; where?

STROBILUS I have found a large pot full of gold!

LYCONIDES What?! What *have* you done?!

(*aside*) He's stolen Euclio's gold!

(*to Strobilus*) Where is this gold?

STROBILUS I've put it safely in a chest at home.

Now I'd like you to set me free from my slavery.

LYCONIDES (*seizing Strobilus by the throat*) Set you free, you thieving slave?!

STROBILUS (*with forced laughter*) Ha ha ha! Nearly had you fooled there master. What would you do if I really had found it? Ha ha ha!

LYCONIDES It's no good pretending now. Give me the gold!

STROBILUS You want me to give you the gold?

LYCONIDES Yes I do: so that I can give it back to Euclio.

STROBILUS Now where am I to find his gold?

LYCONIDES You've just said you've put it in a chest.

STROBILUS Just my little joke.

LYCONIDES Are you now saying you don't have the gold?

STROBILUS Exactly.

LYCONIDES (*seizing Strobilus again*)

Perhaps a good flogging would produce it!

STROBILUS By Hercules, you could kill me, and it wouldn't produce anything at all!

[*Only fragments of the remainder of the final scene are extant.*

Words and lines completing gaps in the text are presented in this typeface.]

LYCONIDES On the whole, Strobilus, it would be a shame to kill you after what I paid for you! So let's go home and see if we can find that chest!

(Exit Lyconides *leading* Strobilus *down the street)*

[5.2]
(Enter Phaedria *from Euclio's house)*

PHAEDRIA I have given thanks to Juno Lucina, Goddess of Childbirth, for the safe delivery of a healthy son. My baby now lies asleep, unaware of the joy he has brought me and of the problems he has caused.

My father tells me I was to have been married to our next door neighbour Megadorus, the only man who would marry me without a dowry. But now that he has learnt of my baby, the marriage has been called off. I've given thanks to all the Gods and Goddesses for that as well: who would want to be married to an old man like that? Particularly when I have someone else in mind! The father of my child is the husband I want! I know so little of him; but when I met him at the festival, I knew he was the man for me: he was good looking, he made me laugh and he said he was from a very good family as well (although I've no idea which one). I don't suppose I've any chance of meeting him again. He's probably forgotten all about me.

And as for my father, he's in a furious temper. He's had something stolen and he's lost my marriage as well. I hope he calms down soon. After all, instead of my looking forward to a wedding dress for my marriage and new clothes for married life ahead with my husband, I'll be living in the same house with him for a long time indeed.

I have my son, but otherwise my prospects are bleak. Where can I find help? Today I have prayed, as I have prayed every day, to our Spirit of the Hearth. I have burnt incense and poured a libation of wine and asked him for help and protection. What other hope do I have?

(*Enter* Spirit of the Hearth *mysteriously*)

SPIRIT What other hope do you need?
PHAEDRIA Who are you?
SPIRIT   Phaedria, don't you know me? You have prayed to me often enough and I have been most grateful for your gifts. I am the Spirit of your Hearth (*indicates Euclio's house*).
PHAEDRIA I feel I know you, Spirit!
SPIRIT You have prayed to me often enough.
PHAEDRIA Spirit, can you really help me?
SPIRIT I have watched over you for many years and I will not fail you now.
PHAEDRIA If ever I needed help, that time is now.

(*Enter* Lyconides *from along the street, carrying the pot of gold under his cloak*)

SPIRIT First of all, I perceive you wish to meet the father of your child.
PHAEDRIA I want that more than anything else!
SPIRIT (*looking down the street*) Well, here he is, coming along the street now!
LYCONIDES (*aside*) That fool of a slave of mine will rue the day he fleeced Euclio of his gold!

71

(*revealing the pot of gold*) It didn't take much finding; he'd hidden it exactly where he said he had. And here it is.

I'll give it back to Euclio. When he has this back, he might be in a better frame of mind and a little more receptive to my proposal.

SPIRIT　(*to Phaedria*) Is this the man you wanted to see?

PHAEDRIA It most certainly is!

(*to Lyconides*) Er..excuse me…

LYCONIDES Yes?

PHAEDRIA Are you visiting my father Euclio?

LYCONIDES　　(*immediately recognising Phaedria*) Phaedria!

I've wanted to see you and speak to you for so long!

(*Phaedria and Lyconides look to embrace, but Lyconides feels he has to keep his hands on the pot of gold*)

This pot of gold seems to be coming between us!

But now I hear you have borne my son; is he well? Are you well?

PHAEDRIA　We are both well; and all the better for seeing you. But what are you doing with that pot of gold?

And why are you here?

LYCONIDES First of all, my son – where is he?

PHAEDRIA　He's being looked after by our old housekeeper, Staphyla. He sounds to be asleep. He's a fine boy!

Now do tell me: what are you doing here?

LYCONIDES I have two purposes; and I hope one will help the other. Firstly, I am returning this gold to your father. It was stolen by my slave, Strobilus, who has found himself considerably mistaken in thinking he could use it to buy his freedom. In bringing it back, I'm hoping your father might have a higher opinion of me than he has at present. This brings me to my second purpose, which is to ask him to give you to me in marriage.

PHAEDRIA (*excitedly*) Do you think he will?

(*less excitedly*) He might do, to get me off his hands. But don't expect a dowry: he'll drive a hard bargain.

LYCONIDES Let's have his consent for our marriage first, and worry about the dowry later. I shall simply try to avoid paying *him*.

SPIRIT I think you father is coming out now.

(*Enter* Euclio *from his house in a state of agitation*)

EUCLIO Time is passing and no sign of my pot of gold! No report of the thief! Nothing! To think of the years wasted in watching over my treasure for it simply to be taken from under my nose!

(*seeing Lyconides*) And what are you doing here?! Haven't you caused enough trouble?! Be off with you!

LYCONIDES (*revealing the pot of gold*) Don't you want this then?

EUCLIO What!! What are you doing with that?

(Euclio *seizes the pot of gold*)

LYCONIDES I have recovered it from the thief and brought it back to you.

EUCLIO You stole it, didn't you?!

LYCONIDES If I'd stolen it, I wouldn't be bringing it back.

SPIRIT He's telling the truth, Euclio. His slave stole it, but Lyconides here, being the gentleman he is, is ensuring that the gold is returned to its proper owner.

EUCLIO (*to the Spirit*) By the Gods, who are you?!

SPIRIT Not being recognised by you is a burden I've had to bear for many a year. I am the Spirit of your Hearth; and, may I say, it is not always the warmest of hearths. Indeed, if it were not for the devotions of your daughter here, I would be a sorry Spirit indeed.

EUCLIO Be that as it may! But how do you know he's telling the truth?

SPIRIT You may be an ungrateful miser, Euclio, but I have still been watching over you. That is what we Spirits do! And you may rest assured that Lyconides here is no thief and that he is returning your gold.

EUCLIO Well, I have my gold now – and that means one half of my problems has been solved. If you all don't mind, I'll take it indoors – by myself.

(*Euclio starts to go into his house*)

SPIRIT A moment, Euclio!

(*Euclio turns to listen*)

SPIRIT You may remember that the last time you saw Lyconides, he was asking you a question.

EUCLIO I remember him telling me he had ruined my daughter's marriage prospects!

LYCONIDES I was actually trying to suggest that I marry her!

EUCLIO (*seeing an opportunity to solve his second problem*)
There'll be no dowry!

LYCONIDES I'm not asking for one.

EUCLIO (*bolder*) Indeed, there could be a matter of damages!

LYCONIDES The truth is, I can't afford to marry your daughter, care for our son and pay damages as well – even if I do deserve to!

PHAEDRIA Father! Dear father! You can see that Lyconides is a fine young man and that we are in love and that he will make an excellent father of our child. Do consent to our marriage – and let us forget about dowries and damages!

EUCLIO Very well – but definitely no dowry!

SPIRIT Excellent!
But Euclio, what are you going to do with that gold?

EUCLIO Mind you own business!

SPIRIT I suggest that you intend to dig a hole and bury it.

EUCLIO How interesting!

SPIRIT Why do you not spend it?

EUCLIO It won't do me much good if I've spent it!

SPIRIT What good will it do you if you bury it?

EUCLIO (*pausing to think about this before answering*)
Well, er, I can always dig it up again if I need it.

SPIRIT But you never have dug it up when you've needed it.
Have you lived an easy life, because of your gold?

EUCLIO Indeed I have not! I used to dig ten trenches a day when I was a younger man and had to make ends meet.

SPIRIT Have your neighbours or colleagues thought better of you because of your wealth?

EUCLIO Of course not! I've gone to the greatest lengths to ensure no-one knows about it!

SPIRIT To such lengths, in fact, that the whole of Athens thinks you're a tight-fisted old skinflint, who would rather chase the cooks away from your daughter's marriage than enjoy a celebratory meal, who would rather wear rags than buy a new tunic – and who is so miserly that he would rather see his daughter unmarried than give her a dowry!

EUCLIO (*to the audience, pleadingly*) Er..look here...It's not that I'm mean: it's just that I don't want my gold stolen.

SPIRIT Would you not prefer for a load to be taken off your mind?

EUCLIO (*to the Spirit*) In what way?

SPIRIT Why not give the gold as a dowry for your daughter?

EUCLIO What!?

SPIRIT In that way, you will be able to stop worrying about it; you will immediately gain a reputation for generosity; and your daughter, her husband and their child will begin their new family life together in security.

EUCLIO Spirit, you seem to exercise some supernatural influence over me. Whilst your suggestion is as welcome as a plateful of raw vegetables for dinner, nevertheless, you spice it with some irresistible sauce. Strangely, I find myself agreeing with you!

76

(*To Phaedria and Lyconides*) Come here, you two. Today you shall be married and I will give you this pot of gold as a dowry...

LYCONIDES Thank you, sir. (*reaches out for the pot of gold*)

EUCLIO (*firmly retaining the pot*) ....after the ceremony has taken place.
I shall entrust it in the meantime to our excellent Spirit.
(*Euclio gives the pot to the Spirit of the Hearth*)
Now where are those cooks? Where are those flute-girls? Summon my neighbours to the feast!

(*Enter the* Whole Cast [not already on stage] *from their respective houses or along the street, in festive mood.*)

EUCLIO Ladies and Gentlemen, cooks and slaves! May I announce that my daughter Phaedria is to marry Lyconides; and I have given them a handsome dowry – as they deserve!

(*Megadorus, Eunomia and Staphyla congratulate Phaedria and Lyconides; the Cooks, Flute-girls, Pythodicus and Strobilus bring on the food and make preparations for the wedding.*)

EUCLIO (*to the audience*) I feel so much better already: I never had a moment's rest, night or day, whilst I watched over that pot of gold; but now I'll be able to sleep at night.
(*to the rest of the cast*) Now, go and prepare yourselves for the wedding feast – which will begin as soon as our excellent cooks can prepare it!

(*Exeunt* All *to their appropriate houses except* Spirit of the Hearth)

EPILOGUE
(*spoken by the* Spirit of the Hearth)

> Old Euclio has seen the error of his ways and the pot of gold will be put to good use at last – I'll see to that!
> Megadorus will soon find himself another wife – a young one of course – and as for Phaedria and Lyconides, well, they will live happily and bring up a huge family and still have time to look after their old Dad.
> To end this play, then, Audience, it simply remains for you to give us a round of applause.

(*Exit* Spirit of the Hearth *into Euclio's house*)

www.ingramcontent.com/pod-product-compliance
Lightning Source LLC
Chambersburg PA
CBHW070305290526
45791CB00003B/1089